Who Am I REALLY?

Excerpt taken from my book,
"A Glorious Church"

CLEVELAND O. MCLEISH

Copyright © 2016 Cleveland O. McLeish

All rights reserved. No portion of this book may be reproduced, stored in a retrieval system, or transmitted in any form or by any means, mechanical, electronic, photocopying, recording, or otherwise, without written permission from the publisher.

ISBN: 978-1-63308-193-2

Who Am I REALLY?

WHO AM I REALLY?

"I hear the Spirit of the Lord say,
'You are a son of God!'"

When this revelation came, I was blown away. Somehow a lot of things just started to make sense. It was not just a message for me, but for the world. This is a message for you. So, if you are ready to know who you really are, then read on.

I have never been the kind to simply accept what other people say. I realized very early on that the Bible is open to various interpretations, and often we accept what makes sense to us, and preach that as a settled doctrine. Later, when new revelations come, we are hesitant to let go of old beliefs because that would cause us to face our shortcomings as human beings who are prone to error. No one wants to admit that they were wrong. You also need to know as well that God cannot be confined in a box. If you ever pin Him down to doing something a particular way, He will simply change the way He does it. That is why *revelation* is so important. Proverbs 29:18 says, *"Where there is no vision [no **revelation** of God and His word], the people are unrestrained (perish)…"* (AMP)

> Revelation will always come to the one who is not afraid to admit that what they believed was wrong.

I have always had a problem Genesis 6:2 & 4 – "That the **sons of God** saw the daughters of men that they were fair, and they took them wives of all which they chose. There were giants in the earth in those days; and also after that, when the **sons of God** came in unto the daughters of men, and they bare children to them, the same became mighty men which are of old, men of renown."

Several red flags go up when I read this scripture. The most obvious question is, "Who are **sons of God**?" It is a crucial question that has been answered for centuries by many respected biblical scholars who claim that **sons of God** are 'angels' or 'fallen angels.' I had several issues with that answer. Firstly, the Bible has never been hesitant to refer to angels as angels, so why on this particular and seemingly isolated instance would the Word refer to angels as **sons of God?** The second issue I have, and the most relevant, is that angels or demons cannot reproduce with humans. To put it bluntly, a spirit cannot ejaculate human sperm to impregnate a woman. Humans have the capacity to reproduce, not angels.

With that said, there is a thick cloud of mystery surrounding **'sons of God.'** I found it interesting that the term **'sons of God'** appears only eight other times in scripture, six of which are in the New Testament:

> Job 1:6 – *"Now there was a day when the **sons of God** came to present themselves before the Lord, and Satan came also among them."*

> Job 2:1 – *"Again there was a day when the **sons of God** came to present themselves before the Lord, and Satan came also among them to present himself before the Lord."*

> Job 38:7 – *"When the morning stars sang together, and all the **sons of God** shouted for joy?"*

> St. John 1:12 – *"But as many as received him, to them gave he power to become the **sons of God**, even to them that believe on his name."*

> Romans 8:14 – *"For as many as are led by the Spirit of God, they are the **sons of God**."*

Romans 8:19 – *"For the earnest expectation of the creature waiteth for the manifestation of the **sons of God**."*

Philippians 2:15 – *"That ye may be blameless and harmless, the **sons of God**, without rebuke, in the midst of a crooked and perverse nation, among whom ye shine as lights in the world."*

1 John 3:1 – *"Behold, what manner of love the Father hath bestowed upon us, that we should be called the **sons of God**: therefore the world knoweth us not, because it knew him not."*

1 John 3:2 – *"Beloved, now we are the **sons of God**, and it doth not yet appear what we shall be: but we know that, when he shall appear, we shall be like him; for we shall see him as he is."*

Bear in mind that previous interpretations, (or what I was asked to believe), were that in the Old Testament '**sons of God**' were fallen angels, and in the New Testament '**sons of God**' refers to humans. That's not a very reliable approach to Biblical interpretation. To know the truth, we sometimes have to travel back to the beginning.

Armed with all my confusion, and revelation received from others, I went to take a look, and what I found was surprising (to say it mildly).

> Genesis 1:1 – *"In the beginning God created the heaven and the earth."*

What we read in Genesis Chapter 1 has always been attributed to, by and large, what was happening in the earth, in the natural, but let's take a closer look.

> Genesis 1:26 – *"And God said, let us make man in our image, after our likeness: and let them have dominion over the fish of the sea, and over the fowl of the air, and over the cattle, and over all the earth, and over every creeping thing that creepeth upon the earth."*

> Genesis 1:27 – *"So God created man in his own image, in the image of God created he him; male and female created he them."*

What I found interesting was that when we get to Genesis 2:5 it says, "And every plant of the field before it was in the earth, and every herb of the field before it grew: for the Lord God had not caused it to rain upon the earth, and **there was not a man to till the ground."**

You will understand that by this time I was utterly confused, but what I missed, and I believe the Lord pointed this out to me, was that before there was anything on the earth, it had to be created first in the heavens. That is why we read… *"and God created the heavens and the earth."*

> Genesis 1:27 – *"So God created man in his own image, in the image of God created he him; male and female created he them."*

This is where it starts to get more interesting, because both male and female were created in the image and likeness of God, so we looked like God. We bore His resemblance. Note also that both male and female were created before God formed man from the dust, and before Eve was taken out of Adam, that is if you read the sequence of events in chronological order (yes, I realize that Hebrew writings are not chronological). Theologians will say that Genesis 1 is a summary, and Genesis 2 expands on the summary. If that was true, both chapters actually read like a summary, so there would be some overlapping that makes little sense.

> Genesis 2:7 – *"And the Lord God planted a garden eastward in Eden; and there he put the man whom he had formed."*

In Genesis 2, everything that God created in the realm of the spirit took form in the natural, including man and woman. We were spirit (Genesis 1), soul and body (Genesis 2), and we looked like God, so our spirit man, which is who we are, was on the outside, and we were much bigger than our human form. Personally (and this is me, not necessarily the Lord) I don't think Adam and Eve had to climb a tree to pick and eat its fruit. This was also why it was possible for them to be 'naked and unashamed' (Genesis 2:25). I have heard it said by theologians that a celestial light covered man. It was not just light, but their spirit (who they really were – who we really are).

The dynamics of man, however, changed when we sinned, and before we started to reproduce. When man sinned, spiritual death occurred leaving our bodies exposed, and handing the reign of rule over to our souls. Man should be led by the spirit, not the soul.

> 1 Thessalonians 5:23 – *"May God himself, the God of peace, sanctify you through and through. May your whole*

> <u>*spirit, soul and body*</u> *be kept blameless at the coming of the Lord Jesus Christ."*

The enemy wants us to believe that we are a body with a soul and spirit deep inside when the truth is we are a spirit being with a soul and body. Always leave it to the enemy to do a 180 degree flip on any truth.

Look at this absorbing verse:

> Genesis 5:3 – *"And Adam lived an hundred and thirty years, and begat a son in his own likeness, after his image; and called his name Seth."*

Mankind no longer resembled God but became a reflection of our fallen natural man. We were a body with a soul and a dormant spirit. In essence, we really died (not a physical death) on that day Adam and Eve disobeyed God and fell into sin.

So here is the truth about who you really are. As a spirit being, you were initially a **son of God** who stood before the throne of

God, even shouted for joy when stars began to sing before His throne (Job 38:7). Every human being was a **son of God** before being conceived in this world. You were a **son of God** before conception, and it doesn't matter the circumstance that brought you here.

> Jeremiah 1:5 – *"Before I formed thee in the belly I knew thee; and before thou camest forth out of the womb I sanctified thee, and I ordained thee a prophet unto the nations."*

This revelation also explains pre-destination because every human being was pre-destined to be a **son of God** come from heaven to earth. Our names were already written in the book of life as an heir to the throne, but the choices we make while we are here will determine if our name remains, or get blotted out.

> Revelation 3:5 – *"He that overcometh, the same shall be clothed in*

white raiment; and I will not blot out his name out of the book of life, but I will confess his name before my Father, and before his angels."

The fact that your name can be blotted out suggests that it is already written. I shared this revelation with a trusted few, and was shown as excerpt from a book that I want to quote here to make a point:

"Theory of pre-existence - This view, which advocates that the human soul has existed previously, has its roots in non-Christian philosophy; it is taught in Hinduism and was also held by Plato, Philo, and Origen. This theory teaches that in a previous existence men were angelic spirits, and as punishment and discipline for sin, they were sent to indwell human bodies. There are a number of problems with this view: there is no clear statement of scripture to support this view (although

the idea may have been presented in John 9:2); no one has any recollection of such an existence…"[1]

To a very large extent, this theory is distorted truth, particularly the last statement. People undergoing generational deliverance have had the experience of remembering leaving heaven to be born on earth. What is also interesting about this quote is the vague notion of truth embedded in a deception. I have found that is exactly how the enemy has worked from the beginning. He takes the truth and manipulates it to keep us from ever venturing near the truth. Almost everything that the enemy has distorted we have shunned out of fear or mere skepticism. In our state of ignorance, the enemy has established his kingdom here on earth unchallenged and has used almost everything that rightfully belongs to God's children. For example, Philip was taken from

---

[1] Paul P. Enns, *The Moody Handbook of Theology*, rev. and expanded. ed. (Chicago: Moody Publishers, ©2008), 317.

one place to another by the Spirit, after baptising the Ethiopian Eunuch. In God's world, it is called *transrelocation*, and the Spirit of God always initiates it. In the enemy's world, it is called *astral projection*.

If you struggle to see the point I just made, let me use a simple illustration, as this information will help you as we move into the final era of the Gentile age.

Commissioned by God, Moses approached Pharoah and threw down his staff. By God's power, the staff became a snake. Pharoah's magicians did the same thing; the only difference is Moses snake/rod swallowed Pharoah's snake/rod demonstrating the greater power. What we often miss in this story is that the enemy was able to replicate what God did. The enemy knows how the spirit world works, and he manipulates it for his benefit, but he is not the creator of anything. The real and the counterfeit look very much alike, but we need to be able to discern the difference in these last days.

Back to who we are, keeping in mind some very simple truths: we are only born here on earth once, and we only get to live life on earth once. God is not in the business of recycling, so this in no way supports reincarnation.

I had a very uncomfortable experience recently while away from home in a foreign country. My wife and I have been taking communion almost every night for several weeks. We were in the process of meditation and prayer when I suddenly felt my body start to literally enlarge. It was growing big, and very heavy and I thought I was going to die. I could sense the spirit of fear and death in the room but wasn't sure what was happening. No one has been able to explain this unfortunate episode, and that has been my issue with the church for years. I always ask hard questions, but seldom get real answers. In a way, our spiritual senses have not been exercised (through constant use) to discern good from evil. Very often, we can't tell the difference.

When I look around me, I see many people who are sick or are experiencing challenges. We focus on our physical bodies, so we miss the reality of who we really are. Jesus became our sin and our curse to redeem us. As a Believer, our spirit man has been restored, and that should be our focus. As a non-Believer, our spirit man remains dormant, and unregenerated.

> I hear the Spirit of the Lord say, 'Who Adam was before he sinned, is who you are now as a born again Christian.'

As Believers, all that was paid for at the cross is contained within our spirits, and must be released into the soul and body for us to experience the abundant life that the Scriptures speak about.

On the other end of the spectrum, if you have never accepted Jesus as your Lord and Saviour, I need you to know today that you were born to be a **son of God**, not a sinner.

Before you were born,
you were a **son of God!**

Your place is with God, and every possible thing that would keep you away from God is deeply cloaked in deception. The enemy wants you to believe that you are living at the top of your game when in reality he is only robbing you of what is rightfully yours. In essence, you have not yet begun to live.

John 10:10 – *"The enemy comes to steal, kill and destroy; but I (Jesus) have come that you might have life, and have it more abundantly."*

Can you honestly say you are living an abundant life? Or is there a nagging feeling that something more meaningful and fulfilling is missing from your life? I meet so many people who are living a kind of life they don't want their children to live. You have dreams for your kids, and God has dreams for you; everything He has ordained you to be and do is recorded on your scroll.

You may have one pressing question at this point. If you were a **son of God**, a spirit before God's throne before you were formed in the womb, why can't you remember? Several things come to mind when I consider this question. I believe babies are born innocent in the world and can see very clearly in the spirit, but as they grow, their souls become contaminated with sin, pre-conceived ideas and iniquity that lessens, and eventually destroys their ability to see in the spirit, unless they are born again. If babies could talk, a lot of the mysteries we are seeking after now might be solved.

On another note, we have never actually asked the Father to help us remember. People have asked and have remembered. Maybe if you ask, He will grant that request. Also, when we are born again, we are born again as spiritual babes. Just as in the natural, our spirit man will desire the sincere milk of the Word as he grows into maturity. Many Christians neglect their spirit man and are malnourished as a result.

Finally, memory is a soul function. You only became a 'living soul' at conception. Memories are imprinted in your mind, which is attached to your eternal soul. What this means, is that now that you are born, you will never, ever cease to exist, or forget.

In the same way, our physical body must be properly fed and nourished to grow daily, our spiritual man demands the same effort. Even Jesus *grew in stature, and wisdom and in favour with God and man* (St. Luke 2:52). You will also notice that there is something in man that draws us to worship something. There will always be that part of us that knows our true home.

Believers, you were born to be a **son of God**. Rise up and take your place. Everything that Jesus had access to during His earthly ministry now belongs to you. He wasn't just doing it for you, but He was demonstrating what God has placed inside you, and what you can do because of your Sonship (adoption into the family of God). Everything that Jesus did, you can do, and you are supposed to do. That is the essence and purpose of this book, to activate you through knowledge and revelation to begin to walk like Jesus. God can and wants to use you to heal the sick, cleanse lepers, cast out demons and raise the dead. You can pray and see food multiply, water turn to wine, blind eyes see, deaf ears open, the mute speak, the lame walk, and (my personal favourite) you can walk on water.

Non-Believers, you were created for a purpose, and pre-destined to be a child of God. You are a potential citizen of heaven, but this reality is tied to your choices. If you reject Jesus, you reject life. Don't be fooled by the enemy. There is no life outside of Christ. There is existence, that appears to have meaning and substance, but it is empty and lacks eternal value. You have not begun to live until you reject sin, and allow Jesus to make you whole: spirit, soul and body. There is something within every human being that cries out for God. He will do everything in His power to save you from a God-less eternity, filled with torment, absent of love, but the final choice is yours. Will you say yes to Jesus today?

Pray This Prayer

Father, I acknowledge You as the one true, and living God. I acknowledge that Jesus came in the flesh, lived, suffered and died for my sins and now sits at the right hand of God. Please forgive me for choosing my own way. Come and dwell in me, and make me whole. Fill me with Holy Spirit, so I can be empowered to walk and live on earth as a son of God, in Jesus Name. Amen.

Son, go and make your Father proud!

Prophetic Word

Before you were formed in the womb, I knew you. You were with me. I know what you looked like, and how you sounded. I knew you. I have loved you with an everlasting love. If you doubt that, the enemy has planted seeds of doubt in your mind. I know my thoughts towards you, they are thoughts of peace, health and prosperity...to give you an expected end. I have dreams for you, as a father dreams for his children. You are my son, and there are only two types of sons: the ones who stay and the ones who stray, but they remain sons nonetheless. Come to me, and let me show you who I really am and let me teach you who you really are.

Have questions? Need counselling?
Call: 1-876-352-2650

Email: cleveland.mcleish@gmail.com

www.ingramcontent.com/pod-product-compliance
Lightning Source LLC
Chambersburg PA
CBHW052046070526
44584CB00018B/2632